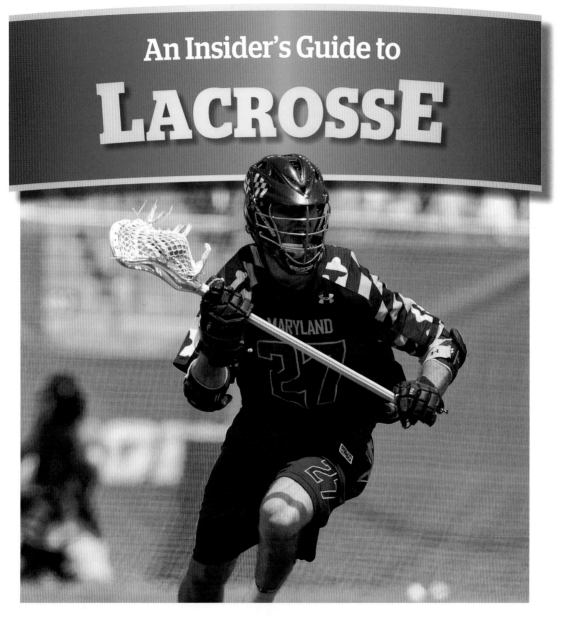

An Insider's Guide to
LACROSSE

CAMERON JONES AND CHRIS HAYHURST

rosen publishing's
rosen
central

NEW YORK

Published in 2015 by The Rosen Publishing Group, Inc.
29 East 21st Street, New York, NY 10010

First Edition

Library of Congress Cataloging-in-Publication Data

Jones, Cameron.
An insider's guide to lacrosse/Cameron Jones and Chris Hayhurst.
    pages cm.—(Sports tips, techniques, and strategies)
Includes bibliographical references and index.
ISBN 978-1-4777-8077-0 (library bound)
ISBN 978-1-4777-8078-7 (pbk.)
ISBN 978-1-4777-8079-4 (6-pack)
1. Lacrosse—Juvenile literature. I. Title.

GV989.14.J66 2014
796.34'7—dc23

2014020384

Manufactured in Malaysia

Metric Conversion Chart			
1 inch	2.54 centimeters 25.4 millimeters	1 cup	250 milliliters
1 foot	30.48 centimeters	1 ounce	28 grams
1 yard	.914 meters	1 fluid ounce	30 milliliters
1 square foot	.093 square meters	1 teaspoon	5 milliliters
1 square mile	2.59 square kilometers	1 tablespoon	15 milliliters
1 ton	.907 metric tons	1 quart	.946 liters
1 pound	454 grams	355 degrees F	180 degrees C
1 mile	1.609 kilometers		

Contents

CHAPTER 1

A History of Lacrosse

Players in helmets running down the field, tightly clutching onto their sticks is a sight you've probably seen often. You've heard them shouting to each other, yelling for the ball. You've seen the moves—the quick stops and starts, the tricky head fakes, the dizzying spins. You've seen this game people call lacrosse. But do you really know what it's all about?

Organized lacrosse has been around for decades. By some accounts, it's the oldest game in North America and has been around for centuries. But it was relatively recently, in the last twenty years or so, that lacrosse finally took hold as a big-time sport in the United States and Canada. Today, lacrosse is so popular that it just may be the fastest growing sport in America.

Lacrosse is a combination of basketball, soccer, and hockey. Agility, coordination, and speed are the most important elements in lacrosse.

Lacrosse is a fusion of several other sports. It combines aspects of popular games like basketball, soccer, and hockey and rolls everything together into one exciting sport. The game is fast-paced, and action moves around the playing field with lightning quickness. Players sprint up and down the field as fast as they can, hoping to score a goal by using their sticks to flick the ball into the opponent's net. The opposing team tries desperately to keep this from happening. Possession of the ball constantly changes as each team struggles to gain momentum.

Lacrosse requires an immense amount of teamwork. Passing the ball between players is fundamental—without passing and cooperation among teammates, it would be impossible to win. Lacrosse also requires commitment. It takes a lot of effort and practice to become good at the game and years of play before skills can be mastered. Lacrosse rarely comes easy—even for the best of players. Consider playing lacrosse seriously only if you're willing to work at it.

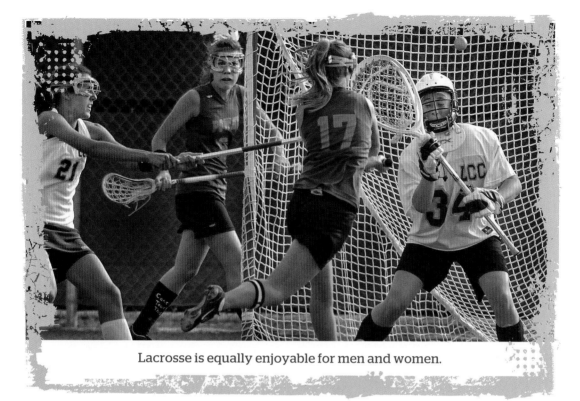

Lacrosse is equally enjoyable for men and women.

What does it take to become a lacrosse player? First, you need to want to play the game. Like any other sport, a passion for lacrosse will make you a better player. Once you get going, it helps to be quick on your feet. Fast runners are rewarded with goals. It also helps to be nimble with your hands—good hand-eye coordination can be the key to scooping, catching, passing, and handling the ball. You have to be in good shape, of course, but that will come once you start playing. The most important thing you need is a good attitude. With the right mind-set, anyone can succeed at lacrosse. Just get out and play!

If lacrosse is the oldest sport in North America, you might guess it has a great history. And you'd be right. Lacrosse has been passed down through the years from generation to generation ever since Native Americans invented an early form of the game back in the fifteenth century. The game we play today has developed and evolved greatly from those humble beginnings into a game enjoyed and loved by thousands of men and women, from grade school children to college athletes to professionals.

The Origin of Lacrosse

Lacrosse was created in the fifteenth century by the native tribes of eastern North America. It was then, and perhaps even earlier (it is impossible to know for certain), that Native Americans began playing a game using sticks, a ball, and some sort of designated goal. Games were played on fields, but the fields used by Native Americans centuries ago were nothing like the fields of today. There were no boundaries. There was no referee. There was only one major rule: no hands. However, over the centuries, the objective of the game has remained the same: put the ball in the other team's goal.

Instead of using their hands, the Native Americans who played this early version of lacrosse used sticks. Southeastern tribes (including the Cherokee) played the game using two short sticks, which were used to carry a ball made

American artist George Catlin, captivated by lacrosse,
painted the Chocktaw tribe playing in 1846.

from deer skin. A slightly different approach was adopted by the Northern tribes located in the Great Lakes region. They used a single 3-foot-long stick with one end carved into a spoon-like scoop. They used the scoop to pick up, carry, and throw the ball. Still other tribes, especially those in the Northeast (like the Iroquois), played the game with longer sticks. They fastened webbing to the end of the stick and formed it into a small pocket in which the ball could be carried.

The game, played primarily by male warriors, was typically played for fun, as a sort of practice to make fighters tougher and stronger. But the game was also used to settle arguments between tribes. Disputes about tribal boundaries or a tribe's claim to hunting grounds were sometimes settled not by battles fought with knives and arrows, but with sticks and a ball.

Before each game, Native Americans held religious ceremonies to honor the players and to acknowledge the spirits they believed watched over the tribes. Between 100 and 1,000 warriors at a time would play from sunrise to sunset, and games could last for days. Goalposts were usually made of two poles, trees, large rocks, or some other objects that would mark the goal. Some of these goalposts were miles apart from each other, creating an enormous goal. The ball was made of anything the Native Americans could find—typically wood, rock, hardened clay, or animal hide. (Today, lacrosse balls are made from hard rubber and are about the size of a tennis ball.) There were also no boundaries to the playing field.

Early games played between the Native American tribes had very few rules, as can be seen in this 1846 painting.

The players ran all over the countryside, jumping over streams and rivers, dodging trees and rocks. They would carry the ball as far as they could before they were overtaken by an opponent or before they became exhausted. At that point, they would toss the ball to a teammate, who would then continue to run as far as he could go before passing, scoring, or losing possession of the ball to an opponent. Not surprisingly, considering the stakes involved, the game was often rough and violent. Many players were hurt. It wasn't unusual for someone to be killed while playing.

Lacrosse—America's Most Popular Sport?

According to U.S. Lacrosse, the main organizing body for lacrosse played in the United States, lacrosse is currently one of the hottest games in town. Consider these facts:

- An estimated 250,000 men, women, and children play lacrosse in the United States.

- The number of lacrosse players nationwide is increasing at a rate of 20 percent each year.

- More than 72,000 boys and 15,000 girls play high school lacrosse.

- More than 25,000 men and 5,500 women play college lacrosse.

- At least 125,000 kids ages five to fifteen play organized lacrosse through youth and recreation programs.

- More than 300 lacrosse camps are organized for boys and girls throughout the United States.

Lacrosse is a popular sport played in schools, colleges, and universities. Here, UNC (in blue) plays against Duke (in white).

A Novel Game

People began watching this Native American game by the seventeenth century. The first European settlers were spellbound by this strange and exciting new game. These Europeans were Jesuit missionaries who had come to America from France to spread their beliefs about God. They had never seen anything like this sport played by the Native Americans. The Europeans were fascinated by the athleticism and bravery of the players, as well as by the speed at which the game was played. Most intriguing to them, however, was the equipment. The Jesuit missionaries thought the type of stick used by the Native Americans looked a lot like a *crosse,* the French word for the staff carried by Catholic bishops during religious ceremonies. Eventually, they began referring to the game itself as *la crosse* ("the crosse"), and the name stuck.

Before long, settlers went from passive observers of the game to active participants. The first non–Native Americans to play lacrosse were probably Canadians from Montreal in the early 1800s. As the Canadians learned the sport from Native American tribes, they applied new rules and regulations they felt were necessary to keep things "civilized." They weren't comfortable with the freewheeling nature of the game—things like the lack of boundaries, the random goals, and the unlimited number of players allowed to participate at any one time. By the mid-1800s, a Montreal dentist named W. George Beers was at the forefront of a movement to organize lacrosse and introduce the sport to the rest of Canada.

Beers and others helped lacrosse to grow quickly in popularity among Canadians. Lacrosse clubs were created, and games were organized and played before spectators. Official rules were established, the number of players was standardized, and permanent goals were created. Eventually, the game became so popular that it was declared Canada's national sport. Soon the sport spread south to the United States and east to Europe as Canadians traveled to other countries to play exhibition games and show off "their" sport. The original form of the game, however, was kept alive by the Native Americans who continued to play the game.

Canadians were the first to adopt and play the game of lacrosse.
Here, the Montreal Lacrosse Club poses for a picture in 1867.

Lacrosse Gets Organized

The Canadian game began evolving into modern lacrosse in the nineteenth century. In the United States, eastern cities and schools established clubs and teams. In 1877, New York University became the first U.S. college to feature a lacrosse team. A few years later, preparatory high schools followed suit. Lacrosse programs for students were established in Phillips Academy Andover in Massachusetts, Phillips Exeter Academy in New Hampshire, and the Lawrenceville School in New Jersey in 1882.

Organized lacrosse has its roots in Canada.
The Vancouver Lacrosse Club poses for a photo in 1912.

Organized lacrosse is now popular all over the United States.
Here, the Virginia Cavaliers play against the Northwestern University
Wildcats in the NCAA Women's Lacrosse Championship.

More teams were formed as the game caught on. Rivalries soon emerged between high schools and colleges. Clubs from various cities traveled long distances to play foes from other states or across the border in Canada. Women's teams were formed in the 1890s. By the early twentieth century, the game had become so popular that the players and others who loved the game decided to create an organizing body to oversee the sport's development. Before long, the United States Intercollegiate Lacrosse League (USILL) was established. The international community got its first taste of lacrosse when the game appeared as an exhibition sport in the 1904 Olympics in St. Louis, Missouri. Until the United States Intercollegiate Lacrosse Association (USILA) was formed in 1926, the USILL continued to act as the governing body for lacrosse in the United States.

The women's version of the game is slightly different from the men's. Less protective gear is required, because body contact is not allowed.

Lacrosse Today

Today, the rules have evolved and equipment has become standardized. Even though the sport of lacrosse is similar for men and women, there are a few slight differences. The women's game remains somewhat true to the game Native Americans played centuries ago. Little protective equipment is used in the women's game because body contact is not allowed and stick contact is limited. Women also continue to use wooden sticks, or crosses. Men, on the other hand, can "check" each other like they do in hockey, using their bodies and sticks to gain position and force opponents out of the way. The men use high-tech and lightweight aluminum, titanium, and plastic sticks. Helmets and padding are also worn for protection in the men's game.

The modern game is steadily growing in popularity, with thousands of lacrosse teams both nationwide and worldwide. In the United States alone, an estimated 250,000 people play lacrosse. Now hundreds of high schools and colleges, both private and public, have lacrosse teams—a huge leap from the half-dozen or so that pioneered the sport back in the 1800s. Tens of thousands of spectators attend collegiate lacrosse championships each year, flocking in droves to watch young athletes battle for top honors in their respective divisions.

Today, although lacrosse continues to be a mostly amateur sport, there are two professional leagues in the United States. The National Lacrosse League (NLL) oversees the indoor teams, while Major League Lacrosse (MLL) administers the outdoor league. Dozens of countries also have National teams, and the world championships are held every year to determine which team is the best.

CHAPTER 2

The Field

Like most other sports, team work is crucial to win a lacrosse game. The objective in lacrosse is clear: score a goal by putting the ball into the opponent's net. The team with the most goals at the end of the game wins. It's not that easy, of course, as there are a few rules and regulations that players must follow, with slight differences between the men's

In women's lacrosse, there are twelve players on each team, whereas men's teams have ten.

game and the women's game. There are also numerous set plays in lacrosse—the type of plays you might witness in a game of football, for example. Players make special, choreographed moves with or without the ball in an effort to get open to receive a pass, to help a teammate get open, or to get off a shot at the opponent's goal. Lacrosse is a complicated game. The basics, however, are easy to learn.

The Positions

In men's lacrosse, there are four major positions on the lacrosse field: attack, midfield, defense, and goal. The men's lacrosse team consists of three attackmen, three midfielders, three defenders, and one goalie. In all, ten players take the field at a time for each team, while substitutes wait on the sidelines to relieve those who get tired or hurt. The women's game includes twelve players per team: six attackers and six defenders. The attack positions include center, right, and left attack wings; third home; second home; and first home. The defenders include right and left defense wings, third man, cover point, point, and goalie. In the women's game, substitutes are also allowed to come off the bench and join in during the game.

The main task of the people who play attack is to score. Attackmen, as these players are called, must stay on the offensive side of the field—that is, the side of the field with their opponent's goal. Attack men possess excellent stick-handling skills so they can make accurate shots and passes. They are also usually the quickest and most agile players on the team so they can make moves around defenders on their way to the goal.

Attackmen practice things like setting picks for teammates. A pick is a strategic move where one player stands still or moves slowly as another player with the ball runs around him or her. The ballcarrier uses the pick as a shield for protection against defenders. The attackmen work together with each other and the midfielders to move the ball around the goal until a hole in the defense opens up and they can get off a shot.

The Calgary Roughnecks (in red) play against the Toronto Rocks (in white) at the Pengrowth Saddledome.

The men's game has an additional position called midfielder. Midfielders are the only players that can roam the entire field. They are offensive as well as defensive players. They are the connection between the defense and the

The offense (in grey) moves the ball into the opponent's scoring zone as the defense (in black) runs in to try to stop him or slow him down.

This high school goalie is ready to make a save by catching the ball in his net.

The offense (in white) tries to avoid a check by the defense (in blue).

offense, as their main task is to move the ball away from their net and towards their opponent's. Midfielders require both — the scoring skills of the attackmen, as well as the defensive skills of the defenders. The midfielders almost always do the most running during a lacrosse game because they have the most ground to cover.

Defenders have the honor of defending their own goal and must stay on their own side of the field. In the men's game, the three defenders carry 6-foot-long sticks that they use to try to knock the ball out of the hands of the opposing team's attackers and midfielders. They try to stop or disrupt any offensive charge and try to gain control of the ball and send it into their opponent's side.

The last player on the team, and perhaps the most important, is the goalie. The goalie's job is to prevent the other team from scoring by being the last line of defense before the goal. Wearing extra padding, the goalie must be both fast and fearless, using the stick to stop the shots of the opposition. The goalie also often acts as the first player to set the offense in motion. After stopping a shot, the goalie often passes the ball to a running teammate, who then begins the attack on the other goal by passing the ball up the field.

The goalkeeper is possibly the most important player on the field. Curtis Palidwor, above, is a famous goalie who plays for the Calgary Roughnecks.

How to Play the Game

Most high school lacrosse games are forty-eight minutes long and consist of four quarters that are twelve minutes each. In college, the games are sixty minutes long, with four fifteen-minute quarters. Players are given short breaks between each quarter and a slightly longer break between the first and second halves of the game. Youth games are often shorter than the high school matches.

Teams are typically permitted three time-outs per game, with a maximum of two time-outs in any one half. The teams change sides of the field after each quarter to prevent either team from gaining an unfair advantage from field or weather conditions.

In the men's game, field boundaries are marked by lines painted on the ground. In addition, a so-called crease surrounds the goal to protect the goalie and give him room to maneuver. This crease is circular in shape and 18 feet in diameter. Only the goalie and his teammates are allowed to enter the crease area. However, opposing players can reach in with their sticks to try to get the ball.

Other field marks include a midfield line, found exactly halfway between the two goals, as well as lines denoting wing areas and restraining areas. The wing areas mark the spots on either side of centerfield where the outside midfielders must wait until the whistle is blown at face-off. The offensive and defensive restraining areas are the spots where the three attackmen and three defenders and goalie must wait until one of the midfielders has possession of the ball following the face-off. Once a midfielder gains possession of the ball, the other players can rush in and join the action.

The women's lacrosse field has no boundaries. There are no lines marking the outer limits of the field and preventing players from running as far as they want. Certain markings do exist, however, around the goal and at centerfield. Unlike the men's game, there is no midfield line that divides the field into two equal halves. Around the goal, there is a crease where only the goalie and her defensive teammates are allowed to enter. An arc, in the shape of a half-circle, is also painted around the goal, but it comes out farther than the crease. During a penalty shot, the players must stay behind this arc.

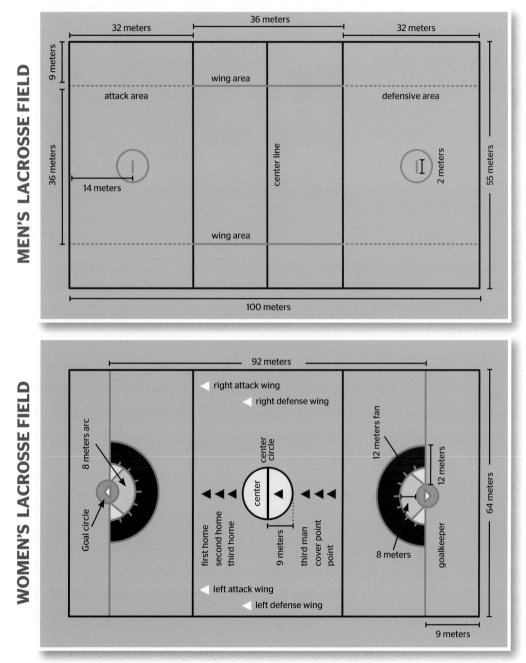

These diagrams show the differences in men's and women's lacrosse fields.

The Blow of the Whistle

A face-off at the center of the field marks the start of the game. An *X* on the field marks the spot. In the men's game, two players crouch down on either side of the *X*. They place their sticks on the ground with the backs of the sticks facing each other. The referee places the ball between the

The referee blows the whistle while the players crouch on either side of the ball to mark the face-off at a college game.

two sticks while the other players stand to the side in the restraining areas or, in the case of the midfielders, in the wing areas. When the referee blows the whistle, the match begins. The two players at the face-off use their sticks to fight for possession of the ball, trying to scoop the ball off the ground as quickly as possible. Meanwhile, the wing midfielders sprint in to help out. Once possession is gained by either team, the other players are released from their restraining areas and the game swings into full motion. The team with the ball begins to move toward their opponent's goal upfield, and the team without the ball defends.

The women's game kicks off differently from the men's game. Two players at the center of the field begin with the backs of their sticks pressed together and the ball held tightly between. The other players stand outside of a large center circle and wait for the referee's signal. When the whistle blows, the two centers push their sticks together as hard as they can as they try to cause their opponent to drop the ball. Meanwhile, the other players from each team rush in from the edge of the circle. Usually, the ball flies high up in the air and possession is granted to the team that jumps high enough to catch it with their sticks.

The Game

The game starts rolling once a team is finally in possession of the ball. Players cradle the ball in the webbing at the end of their sticks by using the force generated by a rapid back-and-forth curling motion of the wrists. This keeps the ball glued to the stick's net even while the players move quickly downfield. The player with the ball runs as far as he or she wants or passes the ball to a teammate who might be open and in better position to move the ball toward the opponent's goal. The player with the ball must, however, be aware of the opposition at all times. The opposing players will do everything they can to steal or knock the ball away. The only way to move the ball is with the stick, as hands can be used by only one player—the goalie.

If the ball goes out of bounds, play stops. In the case of the women's game, play stops when the referee blows the whistle because the ball has gone somewhere he or she deems to be dangerous or too far away. In the men's game, when a ball goes out of bounds or if a player steps out of bounds while carrying the ball, play stops and the other team is awarded possession of the ball. In the women's game, whoever has the ball (or is closest to the ball) when the referee blows the whistle keeps possession. The player must then bring the ball back toward the goals. When a ball goes out of bounds after a shot, the possession is given to whomever is closest to the ball.

This player is receiving a pass from a teammate while members of the opposing team try to catch up with him.

The offense (in white) attempts to shield the ball from the defense (in blue).

Players must take special care to avoid losing possession of the ball to the other team's defenders as they duck and weave their way downfield toward the opposing goal. Defenders have many ways they can take the ball from a player. They can use their sticks to poke, or "stick check," the ballcarrier's gloves and stick in an effort to knock the ball away. In the men's game, they can also hit the ballcarrier with their bodies, delivering a body check in much the same way hockey players do. For safety reasons, these checks must be delivered to the front or side of the player and kept above the waist and below the shoulders. The women's game does not allow body contact between players. Stick checks, allowed in both games, is a common tactic used on any player in an attempt to stop him or her from gaining possession while a loose ball is in the air or on the ground.

The Goal

Lacrosse goals in high school and college games are 6 feet tall and 6 feet wide. Youth leagues often play with smaller goals that are easier for smaller goalies to defend.

As the offense moves the ball toward the opposing goal, they look for an open shot. If they get one off, the goalie tries to catch or block the ball from going into the goal. The goalie uses the huge basket on his or her stick or uses his or her body to stop the ball in the air. Once the goalie has possession of the ball in the crease area, he or she must be left alone and cannot be checked in any fashion. The "keeper," as the goalie is known, then has four seconds to either pass the ball to a teammate or leave the crease area and move onto the open field. If the goalie holds the ball for more than four seconds within the crease, or if he or she steps out of the crease and then steps back in, the ball is turned over to the other team. Once the offense scores a goal, the ball is moved back to the center of the field by the referee for another face-off.

Michael Powell scores a goal for Syracuse against Rutgers at an NCAA match.

The Official Rules and Regulations

Personal fouls may be called and penalties administered by referees in response to inappropriate actions by players to stop the game from getting out of control. When a foul is committed, the offending player can be suspended from play for anywhere from one to three minutes, depending on the severity of the foul. If a referee calls five fouls on any one player, that player must leave the game for good.

Fouls include slashing, tripping, cross-checking, unsportsmanlike conduct, unnecessary roughness, and illegal checking. Slashing is called when a player hacks at an opponent with his or her stick and hits the person anywhere other than on the hands or stick. Cross-checking occurs when a player checks an opponent using the handle of his or her stick instead of his or her body. Unsportsmanlike conduct is exactly what it sounds like: swearing, making insults, and arguing with an official all qualify. Unnecessary roughness may be called if a player uses excessive force or violence on an opponent. Illegal body checking occurs when a player checks an opponent who doesn't have the ball or is not within 5 yards of a loose ball. Other offenses include intentionally checking someone after he or she has passed or shot the ball, checking below the waist, from behind, or above the shoulders, or not keeping both hands on the stick when the check is delivered.

This defender uses his stick to check the offense in an attempt to gain possession of the ball.

The men's lacrosse rules are a lot less stringent than women's.
Body contact, as shown above, is allowed.

A player can also receive a penalty for using illegal equipment. Not all lacrosse sticks, for instance, are legal. If the pocket is too deep or the stick is altered to make it more effective for ball handling or shooting, the player can receive a penalty. Gloves, too, can be illegal if they have been altered by the player to make it easier to handle the stick.

Technical fouls can be called for things like holding, interference, pushing from behind, or stalling. Most of these infractions are self-explanatory. Offsides is another penalty. This occurs when a team has fewer than four players on the defensive half of the field or fewer than three players on the offensive side.

The defender corners the offense, who tries
to retain possession of the ball.

The purpose of the offside rule is to maintain balance on the field, so that all players do not stack up on either the offensive or the defensive side of the field. Screening, another penalty, is called when a player blocks an opponent and prevents him or her from guarding someone else. Warding off is a common foul, called when a player with the ball uses his or her non-stick-carrying hand to block the stick checks of an opponent. Unlike the more severe penalties for personal fouls, these technical fouls result in a mere thirty-second player suspension and transfer of possession of the ball to the other team.

There are lots of other rules and regulations, with variations between the men's game and the women's game, between indoor lacrosse and outdoor lacrosse, and between youth leagues and adult leagues, that are easily picked up on the field. Once you get out and play the game, you will soon be so familiar with these rules and regulations that they will be second nature!

CHAPTER 3

Playing Lacrosse

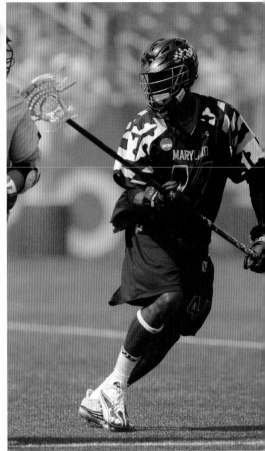

The best thing about lacrosse is its increasing popularity. Youth lacrosse leagues are sprouting up all over the country. Meanwhile, local and regional tournaments are becoming more and more common. Indoor lacrosse—a slightly different version of the game played indoors on either artificial turf or in a gym— can be played all winter long in colder climates. Outdoor lacrosse—typically played on grass—is the choice for those who play in the warmer months. Girls and boys play together in some youth leagues, while in other leagues they have their own teams. Take a look around. Lacrosse is almost everywhere!

Above is an NCAA match in progress in Foxborough, Massachusetts, in 2012.

Lacrosse in College

Many high school standouts go on to play lacrosse in college, whether for clubs or varsity teams. Although both club and varsity teams may represent a school, club teams support themselves through player fees, fund-raising, and tournament fees. Varsity teams enjoy financial support provided by their school. These teams compete with other schools in the region or across the country, depending on the league. The National Collegiate Athletic Association (NCAA) includes dozens of men's and women's lacrosse teams that compete each year for the NCAA championship. Two of the better-known universities with top lacrosse programs are the Johns Hopkins University in Maryland and Syracuse University in New York.

Intramural leagues are also sponsored by many colleges. These leagues are for lacrosse players who may not be interested in playing lacrosse at a highly competitive college level but still wish to play just for the fun of it. Intramural leagues are a great way to stay in shape, play with friends, or rekindle a love for the game. Intramural teams all come from the same college—that is, one college might have ten intramural teams that play each other during the intramural season. One of those teams is crowned the intramural champion for the college at the end of the season.

A lacrosse match takes place in Maryland between the University of Denver Pioneers (in red) and the Maryland Terrapins (in white).

Professional Lacrosse

There isn't much opportunity for lacrosse players to play competitively beyond the collegiate level. There are local clubs and leagues for adults, of course, but these leagues are typically not at the same competitive level as collegiate lacrosse. For players who are outstanding in college, however, there is one option: professional lacrosse.

Professional lacrosse, where the players are actually paid to play the game they love, is a relatively new phenomenon in the United States. The National Lacrosse League (NLL), formed in 1986, is the men's professional indoor lacrosse league in the United States. The rules of indoor lacrosse, or box lacrosse, are completely different from those of outdoor lacrosse.

The National Lacrosse League plays its games during winter and spring.
Other lacrosse leagues play during the summer.

Indoor lacrosse is similar to ice hockey, in that the action takes place inside an enclosed arena. Therefore, it is extremely fast and is highly physical. Currently, there are fourteen teams on the indoor circuit, and the season runs from January to April. Games typically attract between 5,000 and 15,000 fans.

Professional men's outdoor (field) lacrosse is organized by Major League Lacrosse (MLL). Established in 2001, MLL today has eight active teams: Boston Cannons, Charlotte Hounds, Chesapeake Bayhawks, Denver Outlaws, Florida Launch, New York Lizards, Ohio Machine, and Rochester Rattlers. Players, many of whom also play in the indoor league, endure thirty-six regular-season matches from June through September. The best players also take part in an all-star game, an event designed to showcase the skills of

the top players in the world. A tournament to determine the league champion is held at the end of each season.

Dan Marohl is a former player for the NLL's Minnesota Swans. He retired in 2009.

Lacrosse Around the World

The last level of competition beyond the professional leagues in North America is world lacrosse. Teams from all over the planet, including Europe and Asia, gather each year to play against each other and proudly represent their respective countries. These players are the best of the best. They play lacrosse like no one else can.

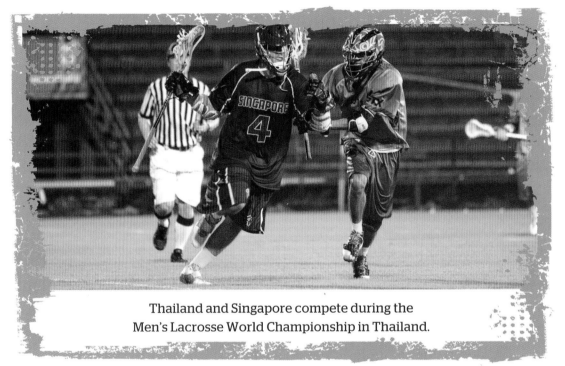

Thailand and Singapore compete during the
Men's Lacrosse World Championship in Thailand.

Every four years, the Men's Lacrosse World Championship was held by the International Lacrosse Federation (ILF), the governing body of international lacrosse competition. In 2008, the ILF merged with the former governing body for women's lacrosse, the International Federation of Women's Lacrosse Associations (IFWLA), to form the Federation of International Lacrosse (FIL). The FIL now sponsors all the World Championships. The United States has won this title almost every year since the competition began in the early 1970s. The United States' only losses came against Canada in 1978 and again in 2006. However, the team was able to reclaim its place at the top by beating Canada at the next world championship.

This dominance is proof of the U.S. athletes' devotion to the game. It also says something about the state of lacrosse in the United States. Perhaps the United States' mastery of the game is due to the abundance of youth leagues. Here, kids can start the game at a young age, learning to master important skills almost as soon as they begin to walk. Or maybe it's the fact that so many high schools now have lacrosse programs, where kids can continue to hone their skills as the competitive level increases. It could be the incredible collegiate lacrosse competition and all the quality players it produces. Whatever the case, U.S. lacrosse is on top of the world, and by the looks of the players coming down the pipeline, it will continue to be for a long time.

Meanwhile, the former International Federation of Women's Lacrosse Association (IFWLA) sponsored the World Cup, first held in Nottingham, England, in 1982. In 2013, the most recent World Cup was held, with the United States beating their host Canada for the championship. Major international championships for players under 19 years of age are also organised by the FIL.

Lacrosse is gaining popularity all over the world.
Here, the National Team of Norway poses for a photo.

The Gait Brothers: Lacrosse Superstars

There is almost no one who has been as influential in the game of lacrosse as two brothers from Canada: Paul and Gary Gait. Their accomplishments on the field have led to the brothers being known as a sibling version of hockey's Wayne Gretzky and basketball's Michael Jordan. The Gait brothers have won almost every lacrosse honor there is to win. They've revolutionized the game like no one before them. The Gait brothers have been, hands down, the most dominant lacrosse players in the history of the sport.

The Gait brothers first came on the national scene as college players at Syracuse University in New York. Playing a game in which they seemed to score at will, the two dominated college play, leading the Syracuse Orangemen to three NCAA Division I championships. Both the brothers played professionally and

Gary Gait is photographed at the NLL All-Star Skills Competition in 2005.

set numerous records. With ten goals each, the Gait brothers hold the record for the most goals scored in an NLL game.

It's impossible to even begin to describe the many ways in which the Gait brothers have left their stamp on the game. But consider these words, as published in the *Calgary Sun* newspaper, from Calgary Roughneck coach Chris Hall, who had the honor of coaching the Gaits when they were teens in Canada: "Both Gary and Paul are the complete package in terms of the prototypical lacrosse player. They have size, athleticism, speed, strength, skill, and intelligence. They're just the whole package." As anyone who has seen the Gait brothers play can attest, these two are the real deal. No one else even comes close.

CHAPTER 4

Gearing Up

Would you like to give lacrosse a try? Getting started is easy. All you have to do is be motivated to learn a great new sport. Give it a try, and you'll be hooked.

A varsity player warms up in his gear.

One of the best ways to get going—or at least to get excited about the sport—is to watch a lacrosse game. Go to a local high school or college and watch one of their games. Or, if you live in a city with a professional team, go see the pros hit the field. You can also sometimes catch lacrosse games on cable television stations like ESPN. Check out the action and see how the game works. You're sure to find it exciting and you'll be anxious to get started playing.

The Equipment

To play lacrosse, you must have the right equipment. Most equipment is required for safety reasons. Additionally, it must meet specific standards.

A regulation crosse for men's lacrosse is between 40 and 42 inches long for offensive players, 52 to 72 inches long for defensemen, and 40 to 72 inches long for goalies. For women, the sticks can be 35.5 to 43.25 inches long.

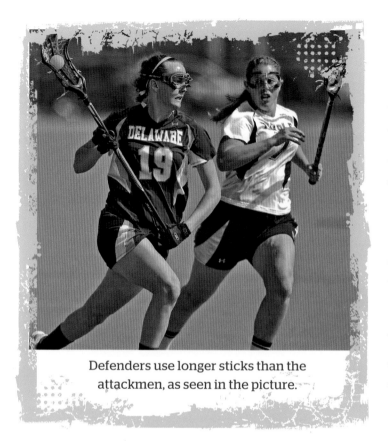

Defenders use longer sticks than the attackmen, as seen in the picture.

The crosse is the main piece of equipment in both the men's and the women's game. These sticks must be a certain length according to the position the player holds (attackmen use shorter sticks than defenders, for instance). The women's crosse has a shallower pocket than the men's crosse does, and in most cases, women are required to use wooden sticks while men can use sticks made of aluminum or titanium if they choose. Visit a sporting goods store or contact a store that specializes in lacrosse equipment. Ask questions and find out which crosse is best for you.

In addition to the stick, women wear mouth guards and, in many leagues, goggles for eye protection. Most players also wear cleats, a jersey, and shorts or a kilt as their uniform. Padded gloves may be worn, but they're not required. Due to the more physical nature of the men's game, men are required to wear a helmet with a face mask, padded gloves, arm and shoulder pads, and a protective cup.

Goalies wear more padding than other players because they must block the ball when it is shot at the net. Women goalies wear a helmet with a face mask and throat protector, padded gloves, and arm, chest, and leg pads. Men's gear is the same, except for the leg pads.

Lacrosse equipment is available at sporting goods stores all over the country, as well as online through several manufacturer Websites. Used gear is also an option, since many people like to "hand down" their equipment as they grow out of it.

The UNC Tar Heels men's goalie makes a save.

Get Out and Play!

Once you discover lacrosse is something you want to try, getting started is as easy as joining your local youth lacrosse league. Most youth leagues are not very competitive because it's just for fun and many of the players are just learning the game. If you find you really enjoy the sport, you can then try out for more competitive teams, like a school team or traveling team. These teams will require lots of practice and dedication, but the rewards will be plenty. Apart from learning the spirit of teamwork, being part of a team will also help you make some great friends!

Some places don't have a youth lacrosse league. If you live in such an area, you might have to travel to join a team. If traveling is not an option, however, you still might be able to play. You'll just have to be ambitious. Talk to an adult who is willing to help out and see if you can organize a youth team yourself. At the very least, you should be able to get a coach and a bunch of kids together once or twice a week to learn how to play the sport. Similar to basketball or ice hockey, lacrosse can start simply through pickup games with your friends in a local park. Keep in mind as you play that lacrosse is not just about winning games. It is a lot more important to let go and have fun!

Youth leagues, like the one shown above, are now fairly common all over the United States.

Glossary

crease A line that surrounds the goal and serves as a buffer zone between the goal and goalie and the offensive players.

crosse The lacrosse stick.

evolve Change slowly over time.

exhibition game A demonstration game, one that is held to introduce the game to an audience.

nimble Making quick and light movements.

penalty shot A free shot at the goal awarded to an offensive player who has been fouled by the defense.

personal foul A foul committed by a player against another player, resulting in a penalty.

referee An official who oversees the game to make sure rules are followed and teams play fairly.

restraining area An area of the field on which certain players must wait at every face-off before joining play.

rivalry A friendly competitive spirit.

stick check A defensive technique in which a player will poke his or her stick at the ballcarrier in an attempt to make the other player drop the ball.

technical foul A non-personal foul called on a player or team as a result of technical infractions, resulting in a penalty.

time-out A short period of rest called for by a team during a game.

For More Information

Canadian Lacrosse Association

2211 Riverside Drive, Suite B-4

Ottawa, ON K1H 7X5

(403) 777-3646

Website: http://www.lacrosse.ca

Federation of International Lacrosse

3 Concorde Gate, Suite 306

Toronto, Ontario, Canada M3C 3N7

(416) 426-7070

Website: https://filacrosse.com/

U.S. Lacrosse

113 West University Parkway

Baltimore, MD 21210

(410) 235-6882

Website: http://www.lacrosse.org

Websites

Due to the changing nature of Internet links, the Rosen Publishing Group, Inc., has developed an online list of Websites related to the subject of this book. This site is updated regularly. Please use this link to access the list:

http://www.rosenlinks.com/scc/lacr

For Further Reading

Hiller, Kelly Amonte. *Winning Women's Lacrosse*. Champaign, IL: Human Kinetics, 2009.

Hinkson, James. *Lacrosse for Dummies*. Mississauga, ON: Wiley Publishing, 2010.

Hinkson, Jim. *Lacrosse Fundamentals.* Chicago, IL: Triumph Books, 2012.

Swissler, Becky, and Katy Bergstrom. Winning Lacrosse for Girls *(Winning Sports for Girls)*. New York, NY: Checkmark Books, 2009.

Tometich, Annabelle. *Lacrosse (Best Sport Ever)*. Minneapolis, MN: Abdo Publishing Company, 2012.

Urick, David. *Sports Illustrated Lacrosse: Fundamentals for Winning*. Lanham, MD: Taylor Trade Publishing, 2008.

Vennum, Thomas. *American Indian Lacrosse: Little Brother of War*. Baltimore, MD: Johns Hopkins University Press, 2007.

Vennum, Thomas. *Lacrosse Legends of the First Americans*. Baltimore, MD: Johns Hopkins University Press, 2007.

Zimmerman, Don, and Peter England. *Men's Lacrosse*. Champaign, IL: Human Kinetics, 2013.

Bibliography

Canadian Lacrosse Association. "A Short History." Retrieved September 2003 (http://www.lacrosse.ca/history.html).

Canadian Lacrosse Association. "The Philosophy of Lacrosse." Retrieved September 2003 (http://www.lacrosse.ca/philosohy.html).

U.S. Lacrosse. "About Lacrosse." Retrieved September 2003 (http://www.lacrosse.org).

Index

Index

About the Authors

Chris Hayhurst has written more than 30 books for middle school and high school students. He has received awards from the American Association of Educational Publishers and the American Library Association.

Cameron Jones writes and edits educational materials from his home in Brooklyn, New York. He was a starting lacrosse player for Williams College.

Photo Credits